SPAIN 2016 HUMAN RIGHTS REPORT

EXECUTIVE SUMMARY

The Kingdom of Spain is a parliamentary democracy headed by a constitutional monarch. The country has a bicameral parliament, the General Courts or National Assembly, consisting of the Congress of Deputies (lower house) and the Senate (upper house). The head of the largest political party or coalition usually is named to head the government as president of the Council of Ministers, the equivalent of prime minister. Observers considered national elections held on June 26 free and fair.

Civilian authorities maintained effective control over the security forces.

The most significant human rights problems included denial of access to asylum and summary forced returns of asylum seekers by police, systemic corruption by government officials, and violence against women and children.

Other problems included the circulation of hate speech on the internet; inequality of opportunity and pay for women in the workplace; subjection of women and girls to sex trafficking; acts of anti-Semitic vandalism; and societal discrimination and violence against persons with disabilities, Muslims, ethnic minorities, including Roma, and lesbian, gay, bisexual, transgender, and intersex (LGBTI) persons.

The government generally took steps to prosecute officials, both in the security services and elsewhere in the government, who committed abuses. In some instances officials engaged in corruption and created the impression of impunity.

Section 1. Respect for the Integrity of the Person, Including Freedom from:

a. Arbitrary Deprivation of Life and other Unlawful or Politically Motivated Killings

There were no reports that the government or its agents committed arbitrary or unlawful killings.

b. Disappearance

There were no reports of politically motivated disappearances.

c. Torture and Other Cruel, Inhuman, or Degrading Treatment or Punishment

The constitution and laws prohibit such practices, and the government normally respected this prohibition. There were reports of police mistreatment; courts dismissed some of the reports.

According to the nongovernmental organization (NGO) Coordinator for the Prevention of Torture, in 2015 there were 128 reports of mistreatment of persons in custody, affecting 232 persons (a decline from 194 reports and 961 affected persons in 2014).

On May 31, the European Court for Human Rights (ECHR) condemned the government for not investigating properly the alleged torture of Beortegui Martinez, a member of the terrorist organization ETA, by four Civil Guard police officers during his detention in 2011.

The constitution provides for an ombudsman who investigates claims of police abuse. From January to June, the national ombudsman filed 494 ex officio judicial complaints, a significant decrease compared with the same period in 2015. In 2015 the Office of the Ombudsman processed 18,467 complaints.

Prison and Detention Center Conditions

Prison and detention center conditions mostly met international standards.

The NGO Pueblos Unidos denounced the conditions found in government-operated foreign internment centers (CIE)--processing centers for irregular migrants--and likened them to prisons. A spokesman for the Ministry of the Interior explained that irregular migrants spent an average of 27 days in the centers.

Physical Conditions: In 2015 (the most recent information available), according to the Coordinator for the Prevention of Torture, 30 persons died in custody.

Independent Monitoring: The government generally permitted monitoring by independent nongovernmental observers, including the Coordinator for the Prevention of Torture and the UN Human Rights Committee, in accordance with their standard modalities.

<u>Improvements</u>: In March the government doubled to 853,500 euros ($938,900) its funding to support additional Red Cross social programs and humanitarian assistance in CIEs. The government also created a monitoring committee to track improvements in CIE service delivery to irregular migrants.

d. Arbitrary Arrest or Detention

The constitution and law prohibit arbitrary arrest and detention, and the government generally observed these prohibitions.

Role of the Police and Security Apparatus

Police forces include the national police and the Civil Guard (both of which handle migration and border enforcement under the authority of the national Ministry of the Interior) as well as regional police under the authority of the Catalan and the Basque Country regional governments. The respective civilian authorities maintained effective control over all police forces and the Civil Guard, and the government generally has effective mechanisms to investigate and punish abuse and corruption. There were no reports of impunity involving the security forces during the year.

Arrest Procedures and Treatment of Detainees

The law provides that police may apprehend suspects for probable cause or with a warrant based on sufficient evidence as determined by a judge. With certain exceptions, police may not hold a suspect for more than 72 hours without a hearing. In certain rare instances involving acts of terrorism, the law allows authorities, with the authorization of a judge, to detain persons for up to five days prior to arraignment. These rights were respected. Authorities generally informed detainees promptly of the charges against them. The country has a functioning bail system, and the courts released defendants on bail unless they believed the defendants might flee or be a threat to public safety. If a potential criminal sentence is less than three years, the judge can decide to impose bail or release the accused on his own recognizance. If the potential sentence is more than three years, the judge must set bail. The law provides detainees the right to consult a lawyer of their choice. If the detainee is indigent, the government appoints legal counsel. There were at times delays of up to several hours between the time a detained person first requested a lawyer and the time the lawyer arrived at the place of detention.

In certain rare instances involving acts of terrorism, a judge may order incommunicado or solitary detention for the entire duration of police custody. The law stipulates that terrorism suspects held incommunicado have the right to an attorney and medical care, but it allows them neither to choose an attorney nor to see a physician of their choice. The court-appointed lawyer is present during police and judicial proceedings, but detainees do not have the right to confer in private with the lawyer. The government continued to conduct extensive video surveillance in detention facilities and interrogation rooms ostensibly to deter mistreatment or any violations of prisoner rights by police or guards.

Detainee's Ability to Challenge Lawfulness of Detention before a Court: Persons arrested and detained are entitled to challenge in court the legal basis or arbitrary nature of their detention and to obtain prompt release and compensation if found to have been unlawfully detained. They may also seek to appeal to the ECHR.

e. Denial of Fair Public Trial

The constitution provides for an independent judiciary, and the government generally respected judicial independence.

Trial Procedures

The constitution and law provide for the right to a fair public trial, and the independent judiciary generally enforced this right. Defendants enjoy a presumption of innocence, the right to be informed promptly and in detail of the charges against them with free interpretation as necessary from the moment charged through all appeals, the right to a fair and public trial without undue delay, and the right to be present at their trial. Defendants have the right to an attorney of their choice. If the defendant is indigent, the government appoints an attorney. Defendants and their attorneys have adequate time and facilities to prepare a defense, and have access to government-held evidence. During the trial defendants may confront witnesses, and present their witnesses and evidence. Defendants cannot be compelled to testify or confess guilt, and they have the right of appeal. These rights apply to all defendants without discrimination.

Political Prisoners and Detainees

There were no reports of political prisoners or detainees.

Civil Judicial Procedures and Remedies

Individuals or organizations may bring civil lawsuits seeking damages for a human rights violation. The complainant may also pursue an administrative resolution. Persons may appeal court decisions involving alleged violations of the European Convention on Human Rights to the ECHR after they exhaust all avenues of appeal in national courts.

f. Arbitrary or Unlawful Interference with Privacy, Family, Home, or Correspondence

The constitution prohibits such actions, and there were no reports that the government failed to respect these prohibitions.

Section 2. Respect for Civil Liberties, Including:

a. Freedom of Speech and Press

The constitution provides for freedom of speech and press, and the government generally respected these rights. An independent press, an effective judiciary, and a functioning democratic political system combined to promote freedom of speech and press.

<u>Freedom of Speech and Expression</u>: The law prohibits, subject to judicial oversight, actions including public speeches and the publication of documents that the government interprets as glorifying or supporting terrorism. The law provides for punishment with imprisonment for one to four years for persons who provoke discrimination, hatred, or violence against groups or associations for racist, anti-Semitic, or other references to ideology, religion or belief, family status, membership within an ethnic group or race, national origin, sex, sexual orientation, illness, or disability.

In July the Supreme Court ruled that hate speech is not a protected right.

Internet Freedom

The government did not restrict or disrupt access to the internet or censor online content, and there were no credible reports that the government monitored private online communications without appropriate legal authority. The International Telecommunications Union reported that 28 percent of the population had fixed broadband subscriptions to the internet and that 79 percent of the population used the internet. Authorities monitored websites for material containing hate speech, anti-Semitism, and terrorism.

To mitigate racism and xenophobia on the internet, in January the University of Barcelona's project Preventing, Redressing, and Inhibiting Hate Speech in new Media, and the United National Interregional Crime and Justice Research Institute cohosted a training course for law enforcement and legal entities in Barcelona. The event focused on the rise of discrimination and hate crimes, existing legislation to address it, and ways to investigate these crimes and protect victims.

Academic Freedom and Cultural Events

There were no government restrictions on academic freedom or cultural events.

b. Freedom of Peaceful Assembly and Association

Freedom of Assembly

The constitution and the law provide for the freedoms of assembly, and the government generally respected these rights.

In July 2015 the government adopted a new public security law that includes fines of up to 600 euros ($660) for failing to notify authorities about peaceful demonstrations in public areas, up to 30,000 euros ($33,000) for protests resulting in "serious disturbances of public safety" near parliament and regional government buildings, and up to 600,000 euros ($660,000) for unauthorized protests near key infrastructure.

Freedom of Association

The constitution and law provide this right, and the government generally respected it.

c. Freedom of Religion

See the Department of State's *International Religious Freedom Report* at www.state.gov/religiousfreedomreport/.

d. Freedom of Movement, Internally Displaced Persons, Protection of Refugees, and Stateless Persons

The law provides for freedom of internal movement, foreign travel, emigration, and repatriation, and the government generally respected these rights. The government cooperated with the Office of the UN High Commissioner for Refugees and other humanitarian organizations in providing protection and assistance to refugees, asylum seekers, stateless persons, and other persons of concern.

Protection of Refugees

Access to Asylum: The law provides for the granting of asylum or refugee status, and the government has established a system for providing protection to refugees. Authorities review asylum petitions individually, and there is an established appeals process available to rejected petitioners. The law permits any foreigner in the country who is a victim of gender-based violence or of trafficking in persons to file a complaint at a police station without fear of deportation, even if that individual is in the country illegally. On July 1, in a letter to Minister of the Interior Jorge Fernandez Diaz, the Council of Europe's commissioner for human rights, Nils Muiznieks, noted video reports of summary expulsions from Ceuta to Morocco on June 4 and 18. He referred to comments he made to the ECHR in November 2015 about "an established practice" of summary expulsions to Morocco from Melilla. Muiznieks expressed concern that an amendment to the Aliens Act sought to provide a "legal underpinning" in Ceuta and Melilla for these actions.

Potential asylum seekers were able effectively to exercise their right to petition authorities. During the year authorities granted political asylum to two gay Moroccan citizens.

Safe Country of Origin/Transit: Under EU law the country considers all other countries in the Schengen area, the EU, and the United States to be safe countries of origin. The government suspended the application of the EU's Dublin III regulation, by which asylum seekers who enter the country through other Schengen countries are liable for return to the country of first entry into the Schengen area under the EU's Dublin III regulation.

Access to Basic Services: According to Amnesty International, the Center for the Temporary Accommodation of Migrants in Melilla was "severely overcrowded." In Melilla asylum-seekers usually waited at least two months, or even several months in some cases, before being transferred to mainland Spain; in Ceuta the waiting period was longer, according to Amnesty International.

Almost 750,000 irregular migrants lived in the country without adequate access to health care.

Durable Solutions: The government accepted refugees for relocation and resettlement and provided protections with the assistance of NGOs such as the Spanish Commission for Refugee Assistance. In November 2015 the government agreed to relocate 15,888 refugees from Greece and Italy to the country by September 2017. The government also agreed to resettle 1,449 refugees from July 2015 to July 2017 as part of the EU-Turkish agreement.

The government assisted in the safe, voluntary return of failed asylum seekers and migrants to their homes.

Temporary Protection: The government also provided temporary protection to individuals who may not qualify as refugees and provided subsidiary protection to approximately 800 persons in 2015.

Stateless Persons

In 2015 the government granted stateless status to 1,151 individuals, most of whom were from the Tinduf Saharaui camps in Algeria. The law provides a path to citizenship for stateless persons.

Section 3. Freedom to Participate in the Political Process

The constitution provides citizens the ability to choose their government in free and fair periodic elections held by secret ballot and based on universal and equal suffrage.

Elections and Political Participation

Recent Elections: All national observers considered national elections on June 26 free and fair.

Participation of Women and Minorities: No laws limit the participation of women and members of minorities in the political process, and they participated.

Section 4. Corruption and Lack of Transparency in Government

The law provides criminal penalties for corruption by officials, and the government generally implemented these laws effectively. Prosecutions and convictions for corruption were rare compared to the complaints filed, mainly because of the extensive system of legal appeals.

Corruption: In January the country's anticorruption police detained former president of Valencia's provincial authority Alfonso Rus and more than 20 other members of the Popular Party (PP) on charges of corruption, money laundering, prevarication, and fraud in an alleged municipal contracts for kickbacks scheme. As of September the investigation involved 47 current and former PP officials, including the former mayor of Valencia, current PP Senator Rita Barbera, and former vice president of the government of Valencia Gerardo Camps. Part of the "Taula" investigation, police also investigated allegations the Valencian branch of the PP funded itself illegally.

Financial Disclosure: Public officials are subject to financial disclosure laws and are required to publish their income and assets on publicly available websites each year. There are administrative sanctions for noncompliance. The Ministry of Finance and Public Administration is responsible for managing and enforcing the law regarding conflicts of interest.

Public Access to Information: The law mandates public access to government information. The government implemented the law effectively.

Section 5. Governmental Attitude Regarding International and Nongovernmental Investigation of Alleged Violations of Human Rights

A wide variety of domestic and international human rights groups generally operated without government restriction, investigating and publishing their findings on human rights cases. Government officials were cooperative and responsive to their views.

Government Human Rights Bodies: The national ombudsman serves to protect and defend basic rights and public freedom on behalf of citizens. The ruling party appoints the ombudsman after consultation with the opposition. The ombudsman was generally effective, independent, and sufficiently resourced; and had the public's trust.

Section 6. Discrimination, Societal Abuses, and Trafficking in Persons

Women

Rape and Domestic Violence: The law prohibits rape, including spousal rape, and the government generally enforced the law effectively. The penalty for rape is six to 12 years in prison. The law also prohibits violence against women, and independent media and government agencies generally paid close attention to gender-based violence. The law sets prison sentences of six months to a year for domestic violence, threats of violence, or violations of restraining orders, with longer sentences if serious injuries result.

According to the government's delegate for gender violence, as of July 26 partners or former partners killed 26 women. The delegate noted that only seven of the women killed had reported abuse prior to their deaths. According to the General Council of the Judiciary, of the 45,955 cases of gender violence prosecuted in 2014, 28,075, or 67 percent of the total, resulted in guilty verdicts. The Observatory against Domestic and Gender Violence reported 33,917 complaints of gender-based violence in the first three months of the year.

National homicide statistics through March--the latest month for which countrywide homicide statistics are available--indicated that gender-based killings represented 11 percent of total killings in the country (eight of 72).

During the year the Ministry of Health, Social Services, and Equality spent 4.8 million euros ($5.3 million) on awareness campaigns across the country, the same amount as in 2015. This spending did not include local government use of the ministry's campaign images printed and disseminated at their own expense.

The Secretary of State for Equality operated a digital platform where units working on gender violence could share information, best practices, and documents. More than 50 offices provided legal assistance to victims of domestic violence, and there were more than 454 shelters for battered women. A 24-hour toll-free national hotline advised battered women on finding shelter and other local assistance. Through June the hotline handled 33,251 telephone calls in Spanish, French, German, Arabic, Bulgarian, Chinese, Portuguese, Romanian, and Russian, approximately 2,500 fewer than in the same period in 2015. In 2015 the hotline received a record 81,992 telephone calls. The website for the support and prevention of gender violence received 41,721 visits as of May 31.

The UN Human Rights Committee report warned that mostly unreported gender-based violence continued to be a problem in view of the high level of violence suffered by immigrant women from North Africa.

Female Genital Mutilation/Cutting (FGM/C): The law prohibits FGM/C and authorizes courts to prosecute residents of the country who have committed this crime in the country or anywhere in the world. Under the 2013-16 National Strategy for the Eradication of Violence against Women, doctors must ask parents in the country to sign a declaration promising their daughter(s) will not undergo FGM/C when they visit countries where the practice is common. Once a family returns to the country, a doctor, who can start legal action against the parents if examination finds that the minors underwent FGM/C during their trip, must examine the girl(s) again. Doctors must also inform the parents of the health consequences of FGM/C.

In July 2015 the government passed the Children Protection Law, which specifically provides for protection of minors against any type of violence, including FGM/C. More than 55,000 current female residents in the country are originally from countries that practice FGM/C.

During the year until August 26, police in Catalonia investigated six cases of FGM/C.

Sexual Harassment: The law prohibits sexual harassment in the workplace, but few cases came to trial. Harassment reportedly continued to be a problem. The punishment in minor cases can be between three and five months in jail or fines of six to eight months' salary. In aggravated cases it can be five to seven months' jail time or fines of 10 to 14 months' salary. The court can increase penalties for victims the court determines may be especially vulnerable.

Reproductive Rights: Couples and individuals have the right to decide the number, spacing, and timing of their children; manage their reproductive health; and have access to the information and means to do so, free from discrimination, coercion, or violence.

Discrimination: Under the law women enjoy the same rights as men. The government generally enforced the law.

Catalan law calls for equal representation in the public administration, coeducation in schools, equality plans for large businesses, and prohibition of the dissemination of sexist content on government-owned media.

Children

Birth Registration: Citizenship is derived from one's parents. When a child does not acquire the parents' nationality, the government may grant it.

Child Abuse: In 2015, the latest year for which data is available, nine minors were killed by either a parent or a parent's partner. As of May the delegate of the government for gender violence reported that gender violence orphaned 10 children. In 2015 the NGO Foundation for Children and Youth at Risk received 369,969 telephone calls and e-mails reporting child violence, a slight increase from 2014.

The Catalan regional ombudsman denounced the poor conditions of shelters housing unaccompanied foreign children in Catalonia, stating that their condition led to frequent escapes from centers and the use of toxic substances (drugs, especially sniffing glue). Approximately 40 children per month arrived (mostly from North Africa), and as of July, 22 percent of the 3,000 youth in the care of the regional government were foreigners. In July the housing for these vulnerable youth was overcrowded by 15 percent. Of the children in the centers, 46 percent said they did not want to be in the centers.

Early and Forced Marriage: The minimum age of marriage is 16 years for minors living on their own.

The law categorizes forced marriage as a crime punishable by from six months to three years and six months in prison. Forced marriage carries similar penalties as coercion. Immigrant groups from the Middle East and North Africa, and Romanian Roma often performed forced marriages. If they occurred within families, they could be difficult to identify and prosecute.

As of August 26, Catalan police assisted seven victims of forced marriage, five of whom were minors.

Female Genital Mutilation/Cutting (FGM/C): Information is provided in women's section above.

<u>Sexual Exploitation of Children</u>: The law criminalizes the "abuse and sexual attack of minors" under the age of 13. The penalty for sexual abuse and assault of children under the age of 13 is imprisonment from two to 15 years, depending on the nature of the crime. Individuals who contact children under the age of 13 through the internet for the purpose of sexual exploitation face imprisonment of one to three years. Authorities enforced the law.

The minimum age for consensual sex in the country is 16. The law defines nonconsensual sexual abuse as sexual acts committed against persons under age 16, and it provides for sentences from two to 15 years in prison, depending on the circumstances.

Penalties for recruiting children or persons with disabilities into prostitution are imprisonment from one to five years. If the child is under the age of 13, the term of imprisonment is four to six years. The same sentence applies to those who seek to victimize children through prostitution. The penalty for pimping children into prostitution is imprisonment from four to six years. If the minor is under 13, the term of imprisonment is five to 10 years.

The commercial sexual exploitation of trafficked teenage girls remained a problem.

The law prohibits child pornography. The penal code criminalizes both using a minor "to prepare any type of pornographic material" and producing, selling, distributing, displaying, or facilitating the production, sale, dissemination, or exhibition of "any type" of child pornography by "any means." The penalty for recruiting children or persons with disabilities for child pornography is one to five years' imprisonment; if the child is under the age of 13, imprisonment is five to nine years. The law also penalizes knowingly possessing child pornography with a potential prison sentence of up to one year. The penalty for the production, sale, or distribution of pornography in which a child under 18 years old was involved is imprisonment from one to four years or up to eight years if the child is under 13.

There is a registry for sex offenders to bar them from activities in which they could be in the presence of minors.

In August, Catalan regional police closed a child pornography ring and arrested seven suspects. Police alleged the perpetrators sexually abused more than 80 boys between the ages of 12 and 17, using drugs or alcohol to incapacitate the victims. They also recorded the sexual abuse and published more than one million photos and DVD videos for more than 300 clients throughout the world. Many of the victims were orphans under the guardianship of the government's General Directorate of Child and Adolescent Care.

International Child Abductions: The country is a party to the 1980 Hague Convention on the Civil Aspects of International Child Abduction. See the Department of State's *Annual Report on International Parental Child Abduction* at travel.state.gov/content/childabduction/en/legal/compliance.html.

Anti-Semitism

The Jewish community numbers approximately 30,000 persons. The descendants of Sephardic Jews expelled from the country 500 years ago have the right of return as full Spanish citizens.

According to Jewish community leaders and the NGO Movement against Intolerance, anti-Semitic incidents continued, including graffiti against Jewish institutions, although violence against Jews was rare. According to the Ministry of the Interior, there were nine cases of anti-Semitism in 2015 (0.68 percent of all hate crimes), down from 24 in 2014. Government institutions promoted religious pluralism, integration, and understanding of Jewish communities and history, but their outreach did not reach all of the country's autonomous regions. In March the Madrid municipal government joined the Declaration of United Mayors against Anti-Semitism, and the mayor of Madrid signed a declaration with the American Jewish Committee that requires the city to condemn anti-Semitism as well as to design school curricula explaining the Holocaust.

The law considers denial and justification of genocide as a crime if it incites violence, with penalties that range from one to four years in jail.

According to a report from the Observatory for Religious Freedom and Conscience, in 2015 there were 187 instances of religiously motivated violence, seven of which instances targeted Jews.

On July 14, police arrested neo-Nazi bookshop keeper Pedro Varela for distributing books that promote hate and discrimination. He was released on a 30,000-euro ($33,000) bond. In an unprecedented ruling, promoted by the Hate Crimes Prosecutor of Barcelona, also in July authorities closed down Varela's bookstore called Europa and his websites. For the first time ever, the court ruled on the criminal responsibility of a business entity.

After a small village changed its name in 2014 from "Little Hill Fort of Jew Killers" to "Little Hill Fort of Jews," repeated acts of vandalism, mostly anti-Semitic graffiti, appeared in the village. The mayor attributed the acts to far-right extremist groups outside of his village.

Trafficking in Persons

See the Department of State's *Trafficking in Persons Report* at www.state.gov/j/tip/rls/tiprpt/.

Persons with Disabilities

The law prohibits, with fines of up to one million euros ($1.1 million), discrimination against persons with physical, sensory, intellectual, and mental disabilities in employment, education, air travel and other transportation, access to health care, the judicial system, and the provision of other government services. The government generally enforced these provisions effectively. Of the 1,328 reported hate crimes in 2015, 226 were committed against persons with disabilities (17 percent).

The law mandates access to buildings for persons with disabilities. While the government generally enforced these provisions, levels of assistance and accessibility varied among regions.

National/Racial/Ethnic Minorities

In February, Interior Minister Fernandez Diaz reported 1,328 hate crimes in 2015, 13 percent more than in 2014. The minister attributed the increase in part to improved data collection measures. Of this total, 505 cases were linked to racism (38 percent), an increase of 6.5 percent from 2014. Catalonia, the Basque Country, Madrid, and Valencia were the regions with the highest numbers of hate crimes according to ministry data.

In its 2015 report, the Office of the Ombudsman reported that the National Police stopped racially motivated police checks but noted that the Madrid Municipal Police continued the practice.

In 2015 the UN Human Rights Committee criticized police profiling, especially of Roma. The report said that immigrants and ethnic minorities faced discrimination in housing, education, work, and health.

According to Fundacion Secretariado Gitano (FSG), one of the largest NGOs working with Roma in the country, 94 percent of Romani children started school at the compulsory age of three, and more than 96 percent of those completed primary education, but dropout rates in secondary education still amounted to 64 percent in 2015, more than double the national average. In 2015, 91 percent of the country's Roma were literate, a gain of almost 5 percent over the previous 10 years. The FSG also noted that, despite many successes, Roma remained marginalized, and they were poorer when compared with other Spaniards due to high dropout rates, poor access to the labor market, and inconsistent use of universal health care. The FSG's 2015 annual report cited 154 cases of discrimination against Roma.

Some of the efforts to address problems affecting the Romani community included tougher penalties for hate crimes, specialized prosecutors, a network to assist victims, and a council designed to eliminate racial and ethnic discrimination.

According to a report of SOS Racism Catalonia, in 2015 there were 442 victims of racism in Catalonia, 310 of which were new victims. The report also found that four in 10 instances of racism go unreported, of which half go unreported at the victims' request. Public security agents perpetrated 35 percent of racist acts, and private citizens 30 percent. Only 20 percent of the victims attempted to access public services such as health care and education.

Acts of Violence, Discrimination, and Other Abuses Based on Sexual Orientation and Gender Identity

Antidiscrimination laws exist which prohibit discrimination based on sexual orientation and gender identity. The law can consider an anti-LGBTI hate element an aggravating circumstance in crimes.

In Catalonia the law provides members of the LGBTI community greater protections than those provided by national law and prohibits discrimination based on sexuality in competencies of the regional government, such as the provision of education and health care. It reverses the burden of proof involved in cases of discrimination in the realms of civil and social law. Nevertheless, the Observatory against Homophobia in Catalonia claimed that homophobia among persons ages 16 to 20 was rising.

The country's consulates enroll in the civil registry of children born through surrogacy.

According to the Ministry of the Interior, of the 1,328 reported hate crimes during 2015, 169 (13 percent) were linked to the victim's sexual orientation, down 67 percent from 2014. The LGBTI association Arcopoli also asserted that most of the attackers were under the age of 30.

The government fought LGBTI hate crimes by sensitizing police and social workers on sexual diversity, increasing awareness of LGBTI hate crimes, facilitating reporting, and providing better assistance to victims of these crimes. Employing a whole-of-government approach, the government channeled its effort in this area through the Spanish Observatory against LGBT-phobia, an initiative created by the Spanish Federation of LGBTI and with the support of the Ministries of Health, Social Services, and Equality, and of the Interior.

In May, Madrid Regional President Cristina Cifuentes announced that the emergency services would provide specialized attention to LGBTI victims.

In March, to fight against transphobia, the Barcelona municipal government created a Trans Service of Shelter and Accompaniment under the LGBT Resource Center of Barcelona. Under this initiative the municipal government developed a guide with information for those wanting to undergo a sex change and resources for those facing discrimination. The guide also identifies LGBTI-friendly projects in the city.

Other Societal Violence or Discrimination

In 2015 hate-crime identifications were up 13 percent compared with 2014, totaling 1,328, according to the Ministry of the Interior. In all, 240 cases involved physical injuries and 205 cases involved threats. Esteban Ibarra, president of the Movement against Intolerance, lamented the estimated 80 percent of unreported hate crimes.

Notably, 23 percent of hate crimes related to religion. Of the 1,328 reported hate crimes in 2015, 70 cases were committed against Muslims (5 percent).

In December 2015 the country's first national manual for the investigation and prosecution of hate crimes was released at an international conference in Barcelona. The manual, which was prepared by prosecutors, magistrates, and academics and coordinated by the prosecutor against hate crimes and discrimination in Barcelona, defines a hate crime and outlines impediments to prosecuting this type of crime.

To improve investigations and to increase the protection of victims, the manual's best practices include increased training for public servants, greater institutional coordination, the updating of protocols, and the creation of more thorough databases of hate crime statistics.

Section 7. Worker Rights

a. Freedom of Association and the Right to Collective Bargaining

The law allows most workers, including foreign and all migrant workers, to form and join independent unions of their choice without previous authorization or excessive requirements. Military personnel and national police forces do not have the right to join unions. Judges, magistrates, and prosecutors may only join bar associations. The law allows unions to conduct their activities without interference.

The law provides for collective bargaining, including for all workers in the public sector except military personnel, and the government effectively enforced applicable laws. Public-sector collective bargaining includes salaries and employment levels, but the government retained the right to set the levels if negotiations failed.

The constitution and law provide for the right to strike, and workers exercised this right by conducting legal strikes. Any striking union must respect minimum service requirements negotiated with the respective employer. Law and regulations prohibit retaliation against strikers, antiunion discrimination, and discrimination based on union activity, and these laws were effectively enforced. According to the law, if an employer violates union rights, including the right to conduct legal strikes, or dismisses an employee for participation in a union, the employer could face imprisonment from six months to two years or a fine if the employer does not reinstate the employee. These penalties were sufficient to deter violations.

Workers freely organized and joined unions of their choice. The government generally did not interfere in union functioning. Collective bargaining agreements covered approximately 80 percent of the workforce in the public and private sectors at the end of the year. On occasion employers used the minimum service requirements to undermine planned strikes and ensure services in critical areas such as transportation or health services.

Although the law prohibits antiunion discrimination by employers against workers and union organizers, unions contended that employers practiced discrimination in many cases by refusing to renew the temporary contracts of workers engaging in union organizing.

b. Prohibition of Forced or Compulsory Labor

The law prohibits all forms of forced or compulsory labor including by children.

The government effectively enforced the law. It maintained strong prevention efforts, although the efforts focused more on forced prostitution than forced labor. Unions complained that the government's resources and inspections were inadequate. The government did not implement new forced labor awareness campaigns. Penalties of five to 12 years' imprisonment were sufficiently stringent to deter violations.

There were cases of employers subjecting migrant men and women to forced labor in domestic service, agriculture, construction, and the service industry. Unaccompanied children remained particularly vulnerable to labor exploitation, sex trafficking, and forced begging.

Also see the Department of State's Trafficking in Persons Report at www.state.gov/j/tip/rls/tiprpt/.

c. Prohibition of Child Labor and Minimum Age for Employment

The statutory minimum age for the employment of children is 16. The law also prohibits those under the age of 18 from employment at night, from overtime work, or from employment in sectors considered hazardous, such as agricultural, mining and construction sectors. Laws and policies provide for protection of children from exploitation in the workplace, and these laws generally were enforced.

The Ministry of Employment and Social Security has primary responsibility for enforcement of the minimum age law, and it enforced the law effectively in major industries and the service sector.

The ministry had difficulty enforcing the law on small farms and in family-owned businesses, where child labor persisted. The government enforced effectively laws prohibiting child labor in the special economic zones. In 2013, the most recent year for which data is available, the Ministry of Employment and Social Security detected 13 violations related to child labor, affecting 13 minors. Penalties included imprisonment for six to 10 years and were sufficient to deter violations.

There were reports that criminals subjected children to trafficking in the sex trade and forced begging, both of which are worst forms of child labor. Police databases do not automatically register foreign children intercepted at the borders, making them vulnerable to exploitation including forced begging and commercial sexual exploitation (see section 6, Children).

d. Discrimination with Respect to Employment and Occupation

Labor laws and regulations prohibit discrimination with respect to employment and occupation based on race, color, sex, religion, political opinion, national origin or citizenship, social origin, disability, sexual orientation and/or gender identity, age, language, HIV-positive status, or having other communicable diseases. The law prohibits employment discrimination on any of the above bases, and the government effectively enforced it. The penalty for violating the law is six months' to two years' imprisonment. While the government enforced these laws and regulations, discrimination in employment and occupation occurred with respect to race and ethnicity, gender, and sexual orientation. The government requires companies with more than 50 workers to reserve 2 percent of their jobs for persons with disabilities.

In 2014 there were 14 labor infractions for gender discrimination, that amounted to a total of 106,885 euros ($117,574) in fines, and another four infractions for gender discrimination of job applicants that amounted to 25,004 euros ($27,504) in fines.

According to School Business EADA, the wage gap in high-level managing positions between men and women was 17.1 percent. Women occupied 11.8 percent of managing positions. Wage gap in mid-level managing positions was 13 percent, while at lower level the gap was of 11.5 percent.

e. Acceptable Conditions of Work

The national minimum wage was 655.20 euros ($720.72) per month, the equivalent of 7,862.40 euros ($8,648.64) per year. For a family of two adults and two children, the poverty level in 2015 was set at 16,823 euros ($18,505) per year. The Ministry of Employment and Social Security effectively enforced the minimum wage.

Minimum wage, hours of work, and occupational safety and health standards were effectively enforced, through the Ministry of Employment and Social Security, in the formal economy, but not in the informal economy.

The law provides for a 40-hour workweek, with an unbroken rest period of 36 hours after each 40 hours worked. The law restricts overtime to 80 hours per year unless a collective bargaining agreement establishes a different level. Pay is required for overtime and must be equal to or greater than regular pay. The law provides for 22 annual vacation days and 14 federal holidays.

The National Institute of Safety and Health in the Ministry of Employment and Social Security has technical responsibility for developing occupational safety and health standards. The law protects workers who remove themselves from situations that could endanger their health or safety without jeopardy to their employment.

The Inspectorate of Labor has responsibility for enforcing the law on occupational safety and health standards through inspections and legal action if inspectors find infractions. At the end of 2014, there were 1,842 labor inspectors in the country. In 2014, 98,801 infractions amounted to 330 million euros ($363 million) in penalties, an average of 3,340 euros ($3,674) per penalty. The penalties were not sufficient to deter violations. Unions criticized the government for devoting insufficient resources to inspection and enforcement. In May, Visa Inc. calculated that the informal economy amounted to 196 billion euros ($216 billion) or 18.6 percent of gross domestic product. According to the International Labor Organization, 69.1 percent of domestic workers in Spain contributed to the Social Security system in 2015, compared with 42.9 percent in 2011.

Through July the National Statistics Institute recorded 277,271 accidents in the workplace. Authorities reported 275,059 of these as minor, 2,044 as serious, and 268 as fatal, down from 281 in the same period in 2015.

www.ingramcontent.com/pod-product-compliance
Lightning Source LLC
Chambersburg PA
CBHW080822280726
48660CB00018B/3568